# A Look Inside a Rare Mind

An INFJ's Journal through Personal Discovery

JENNIFER SOLDNER

© 2014 Jennifer Soldner. All rights reserved.
ISBN 978-1-312-20210-8

# CONTENTS

**SECTION 1 – To Be an INFJ......5**
    Discovery………………....7
    You Feel It, I Feel It……..11
    Logic……………………17
    Selflessness……………..20
    Mask……………………23
    Conceit…………………...26
    Self-Conscious…………..30
    Jealousy………………...34
    Accountability…………..37

**SECTION 2 – The Struggles…….41**
    Fight……………………...43
    Roller Coaster…………..46
    Anxiety………………….49
    Manipulation……………51
    Protection……………...54
    Shut Down……………..58

**SECTION 3 – Everyday Living…61**
    Physical World………......63
    Words…………………..66
    Simple…………………....69
    Change…………………...71
    Procrastination…………..74

Shopping……………..…..76
Telephone Aversion………79
Social Media…………....82
Helping…………………..86
Passions………………...90
Restless……………….…92
Accomplishments…………94
Overthink…………….….97
Blessing………………....100

# Section One
# To Be an INFJ

# Discovery

My entire life was spent questioning myself. I always wondered why I seemed different. Why I could never fit in anywhere. Why I struggled so much emotionally. And most of all, why I could not find anyone who understood.

My conclusion was always the same. Something is wrong with *me*. I felt like I was failing at my life and I could never seem to fix it. I changed my persona more times than Madonna. I tried different faiths. I tried different friends. I even changed my wardrobe as often as I could afford to.

But nothing. I continued to fail. I continued to remain alone, misunderstood by myself and everyone around me.

Until one day, I took a Myers-Briggs Personality test and read the results: INFJ. What does that mean? I researched and researched, read and read, pondered and pondered, until it hit me…

I am not insane.

I am not failing.

I am not broke.

I am an INFJ.

Those four little letters completely altered my existence and transformed my outlook on everything.

I realized I was stronger than anyone I knew, not weak as I had always been led to believe. I realized I had amazing gifts and talents, not oddities and abnormalities.

In four tiny letters, my life made sense.

I cling to those four letters as though they define everything in my existence. No, the descriptions are not always 100% accurate, but the letters still complete me. They remind me daily that I am not insane and that I am different for a reason.

Everyone I know who has taken the personality test sees their four letters, reads their description, finds it interesting and moves on. Most do not remember their personality type after a week or two. I think it is hard for people to understand why I care so deeply and cherish so dearly those letters. They do not understand that those letters finally led me to understand exactly who I am.

Once I learned my personality type, I was able to begin my personal growth and development. I now feel as though I become a better person every day. I know I am not a failure or a freak.

I am an INFJ and I hold that with more pride than any other personality type could ever understand.

In these pages, I wish to share with you my thoughts through the early stages of my discovery: the positive, the negative, the joyful and the depressing. Welcome to the rare mind of an INFJ.

## Words from Other Rare Minds

*"I remember doing the test for the first time at age 16 and realizing then out of a class of 44 people, I was the only INFJ and one of only two introverts. I hang onto it for the same reason. I've felt out of things my whole life but now I do know there are others like me. INFJs and other introverts need to be proud of who we are. And if it helps us to have a sense of our own place in the scheme of things, I don't see anything wrong with that." ~Mel*

"I cling on to these four letters very strongly when I found out I was an INFJ. To remind myself that I'm not insane, strange or weird, but just plainly an INFJ." ~T.

"After 32 years of life, I had always felt like there was a lot wrong with me. That I wasn't normal. That I wasn't like most others. Then I found out my type, INFJ, and cling to those letters as well. It brought such great clarity and understanding to my whole life." ~Kevin

"When I took the test at age 15 I was also confused until I read the description beneath and my life changed. Your type isn't a limitation to what you can be, let it become a beginning point for your growth into something stronger." ~Anonymous

# You Feel It, I Feel It

In my experience, the most misunderstood part of an INFJ is how we feel everything those around us feel. We do not sympathize. We do not empathize. We literally feel exactly what you feel. Even if you are trying to hide it or don't express your feelings, somehow we still know.

The "N" stands for iNtuitive. While there are other intuitive personalities out there, the INFJ is the most intuitive, sometimes to the point of having almost a sixth sense. When there is tension in the room, an INFJ tenses up. When someone is crying, we want to cry. When someone is elated, we are on cloud nine.

Personally, I cannot remember the last time I felt my own feelings, rather I take on what those around me feel. I have been known to gravitate toward happy, optimistic people just for the relief of their emotions.

The weird part is that I don't have to be in the same vicinity as someone to feel their emotions. I can hear a news story, I can read a book, I can watch a movie. I have a hard time with horror films because of how strongly and realistically I feel the emotions of the people on the screen. I avoid the news. I block out negative stories people tell. I skip magazine articles. It is not that I am trying to be ignorant to the pains in the world, but I physically cannot handle the excess of emotions.

For example, if someone on the news is talking about their child being molested, I don't just feel the emotions of the parent talking. I also feel the emotions of the child they are talking about, the molester who brought about the crime, those not mentioned but clearly affected, like the other parent or relatives or the relatives of the molester. Not to mention, I am still feeling the emotions of every other news story in that half hour of television. It can become an extreme overload that has been known to cause physical ailments such as tumors, ulcers, and headaches.

I cannot express how genuine the emotions are. Sometimes it can be frightening even for myself so, as an INFJ, I have a tendency to emotionally shut down. I can suppress emotions to the point I feel like vomiting. I turn off to the world around me and to myself. It is the only escape my brain gets, though it is brief.

This is probably the most secretive part of myself, and I would assume most INFJs because when tried to explain to another personality type, I am often met with judgments and considered insane. I'm not insane. I don't hear voices. I don't see visions. Everything I feel is real...and 99% of the time, is accurate. I can freak people out by explaining to them their own emotions to a tee, even though they have done everything in their power to hide or suppress them.

I suppose you could consider this a gift. It is what makes an INFJ so compassionate, caring and warm. Most times I would consider it a curse, however. It is exhausting. It is lonely. It is painful. But it is my life and I try my best to cope with it. It has led to some pretty severe depression, but luckily I am self-aware enough to continue to pull myself out of it.

So there it is. The hardest part to understand about an INFJ.

# Words from Other Rare Minds

*"I cannot and will not watch reality or fictional shows where someone else is either feeling embarrassed or humiliated. It physically affects me like I'm the one completely humiliating myself in that large crowd."*
~Missy

*"I remember watching a reenactment of the sinking of the Titanic and my mom was shocked at my reaction: I couldn't stop sobbing at the thought of what those people went through and all those lives lost. I was 18 at the time and it was as if I'd been there with them."*
~Lianne

*"I cannot live in a city because I literally walk around feeling 'electric shocks' from absorbing the emotions of people around me. It is just too overwhelming and painful. I pick up positive emotions too, but they are easier to cope with. I have had to learn to 'numb out' at times and put up a kind of shield. The problem with that*

*is it makes me numb to my own feelings as well. I'd rather feel it all than not feel at all."* ~Rebecca

*"Because I feel so much of everything, I have to block myself off. I have begun to act on the idea of pursuing positive people and positive experiences. Having meaningful rather than meaningless interactions is super critical now. Meditation/yoga/mindfulness helps reduce thinking/feeling dissonance, as does art, music, and writing. It has always been hard to find friends who are proactive. Maybe I've just always been on the quest for meaning..."* ~Joe

*"I really thought something was wrong with me because of the intensity of my feelings. My highs were really high and my lows were really low. There are days when I just wish I could switch off my personality because it is absolutely draining to feel what other people do, not to mention confusing when you can go from incredibly optimistic to monumentally depressed just by speaking with someone... But I will say that I love that this aspect*

*of my personality helps me to know what people are needing and fulfill that need." ~Anonymous*

*"I've been plagued by intense emotions all my life, and have often felt like I was literally losing my mind! I wish I could either just fix all the wrong in the world or make it so I can't be affected by it. Whenever I fail to cope, I suffer from sleep disorders, depression, anxiety, stress-induced eczema, headaches and other psychosomatic illnesses." ~Tammi*

# Logic

As I have explained, I feel the emotions of everyone around me. The emotions of everyone I encounter are strong, accurate and completely real. I feel everything as though I am personally living their existence.

But that is all I feel. I only know their emotions. I cannot understand their logic or reasoning. I cannot tell them what is happening in their life. I do not read minds. I do not understand their existence. I only know how they feel.

Since I, like most people, prefer to feel happy, I always try to make those around me happy. In general, while it can become exhausting, it is a fairly simple concept. I do what I can to accommodate those around me and ensure their overall joy. Obviously I am not always successful, but I do my best.

When it becomes difficult is when I encounter people who have skewed notions of what brings happiness. Some people are selfish and ensuring their happiness means hurting others. Some people are twisted, so their happiness comes from things that make me uncomfortable or even scared. Some people are just confused, so their happiness is almost impossible to attain.

I think the most frustrating part is that I feel the emotions of those selfish, twisted and confused people but cannot grasp the logic by which they live. For example, if I read about a rapist, I can feel their emotions of twisted joy, pleasure and power when they accomplish what makes them happy. It is really hard for me to feel those emotions and for quite some time it left me confused as to how I could relate to them. Before I recognized my abilities to feel accurately what everyone else feels, I was disturbed by who I could relate to. I wondered if there was something wrong with me; if deep down I was twisted, selfish and confused.

As an INFJ, it is hard to watch someone in pain and feel their hurt, knowing that I cannot make them happy. It is part of the daily struggle that exhausts an INFJ so quickly and causes our need for emotional down time. But part of succeeding in life as an INFJ is recognizing that the emotions of others are not ours. We feel it, but the logic is not there. We may emotionally relate to a murder or a psychopath, but we do not logically condone it.

It is scary, but we must separate our emotions from those of others and use our own logic to hold onto who we are. We have to remember that we are unique individuals and do our best not to lose ourselves in those around us.

# Selflessness

INFJs have a tendency to be taken advantage of. We are aware of this, but there is little we can do about it. Selfishness is something that we are pretty much incapable of. Allow me to explain.

As I mentioned before, if you feel it, I feel it. Therefore, if I act in a selfish manner, I feel the emotions that causes in those around me, whether it is anger, hurt, or disappointment. In almost every case, a selfish act on my part is not worth the pain of feeling those emotions.

For example, I remember as a little girl my sister would ask me to play a board game. If I did not want to play, I would say no and I would strongly feel her disappointment and longing to play that game. It would tear me apart. At the time, I wasn't aware of my gift (curse?) of feeling others emotions so I would have to deal with it, confused and alone.

Now I know the consequences of being selfish. I feel the hurt it causes in others and I feel the pain it causes in me. I will always say yes to a board game I do not wish to play.

Others see me as the dependable one who can always be counted on to do what they ask. I don't think they purposely take advantage of me. I know they don't realize the burden I carry. To them, I am just the dependable one.

This personality trait makes it difficult for me to balance my life. A boss asks me to do them a favor which requires me to stay a little late or work on weekends. I have to say yes. A family member needs me to be there to listen or help them with a project. I always say yes. A church member needs me to take over a committee because there is a need for a chairperson. I will say yes.

I become exhausted. I become very stretched thin. But I have no other choice. It hurts me to carry it all, but it hurts me to feel the hurt of others if I don't. I cannot win. I will feel pain, so I might as well help others so my suffering is not in vain.

I am not a martyr but I do often feel like one. This is an aspect of my life where I am unsure if it is a blessing or a curse.

# Mask

INFJs are very internally focused. We tend to live in our heads, keep things private and control what the world around us sees. Part of this is intentional for protective purposes, but for the most part we do not even realize we do it.

I have always been considered cold-hearted, conceited or snobbish. I know this is mainly because I have a face of stone. I take in so much around me and process it internally, so even though I am very perceptive, warm-hearted and aware, none of that shows on the outside.

A lot of times I have to wear a mask. This mask is a forced facial response to the situation. My smiles are fake, my frowns are forced and the subtle changes in my eyes are consciously created. I know many personality types rely heavily on facial expressions and mannerisms to read those around them, especially "sensing" types. Because of this, in order to appear "normal" and make them feel comfortable, I have to create the appropriate facial expressions, since they do not come naturally to me.

I can sit through a stand-up routine that is the funniest thing I have ever heard and never once crack a smile. I can stare straight-faced at someone who has lost their child and not shed a tear. I can be verbally abused and attacked and never even flinch.

It is not that I do not feel the appropriate feelings. I actually feel them stronger than most people. It is, in fact, that I process everything internally. I have the best poker face imaginable, as I am sure most INFJs do too. It can look as though I am not listening or paying attention, but I am in more ways than you know.

Do not take this mask as dishonest. When I force facial expressions for the benefit of those around me, they are genuine in that they reflect what I am truly feeling. Sometimes I do not succeed in creating the proper facial expressions and that has led to misunderstandings, but I always do my best to put forward the appropriate face.

An INFJ's mind is a very busy place. I think we are probably the greatest multi-taskers. While we take in more around us than any other personality type, we are also constantly aware of ourselves, always needing to force mannerisms and expressions, and continuously reading how people feel about those forced expressions. It is no wonder social settings exhaust us quickly and we require emotional solitude in order to recuperate.

## Words from Other Rare Minds

*"I find that I am the opposite. I have to be very aware that my facial expression does not convey too much, or give the wrong impression. A slight change in emotion and my face gives me away, and not necessarily a match to what I am feeling/thinking." ~Anonymous*

# Conceit

Snob. That is one word that people have used to describe me since before I can remember. I've been called a snob by family, friends, co-workers, and even strangers.

It hurts.

I am not a snob. I am not conceited. But I can definitely see why people think that I am.

Another staple characteristic of INFJs is that we are often perfectionists. We believe that even if perfection cannot be attained here on Earth, we should still try to do everything in our power to reach it. We are the least structured Judicial personality types because we are always looking for new and better methods to do just about everything in our lives.

I would never condemn others for being less than perfect. We are all struggling in this world to be the best we can be. Though, to be honest, I do look down on those who are satisfied with mediocrity, because I believe that is a large character flaw. If we grow comfortable and satisfied with where we are, how will we ever grow and improve?

Since I am an introvert, I tend to be very quiet in just about any social setting. Combine my silence, posture, and staged movements and you get a stereotypical snob. I see that. I hate it, and I wish I could prove to people that I am not, but I don't know how to do that without letting them get to know me.

The truth of the matter is that the aspects which come across as conceited are actually my personal attempts to make everyone around me happy. As an INFJ, selfishness is not something I am capable of. I want to be nice so people will like me and trust me to help them. People are not comfortable around those they dislike, and that is very clear to me, so I try to be as polite, sweet, compassionate, and caring as possible at all times.

In my experience, people really like me in professional situations because my snobbish-appearing persona is always business friendly and my politeness and manners-overkill are always taken as professionalism. I tend to struggle more in laid-back situations. I am not good at being relaxed and less-than-polite and I am horrible at chit-chat and small talk. I opt for silence instead. Thus, I never fit in and am always considered conceited.

When people think that I am conceited, I realize I have failed at my mission to make those around me comfortable. Yet, if I fall into the mediocrity that makes others comfortable, I feel as though I have failed myself. I believe we should build people up and help them to be better. Discussing our pitfalls never accomplishes this.

It hurts to be considered conceited, but striving for mediocrity helps no one. If I have to be thought of negatively in order to help others feel better, it is a cross I am willing to carry.

I am an INFJ, and if it will help you, you are more than welcome to think I am conceited.

## Words from Other Rare Minds

*"Seeing how other people live as 'mediocre' is about being snobby. But I mean 'snob' in a positive light. You set standards for yourself. Whether those standards*

*come in the form of who you choose as your friends, or as your lovers, or what you do with your free time, etc., they are a form of rejecting what others readily accept.*

*So in that connotation, I don't mind being a 'snob' anymore. I think it hurts me more emotionally to pretend I'm not and fight it – because ultimately we know that we don't set high standards for ourselves to hurt others or make them feel envious – we do it because to not do it would make us mentally unwell within ourselves."* ~Enid

*"I've always felt deeply wounded when I was viewed as a snob, or 'stuck-up' when I was younger. After a period of time, we are the best of friends...but initially they are turned off by my conservative attire and careful manners. I think they assume it's to fit in with society, when in fact it's [because] I LOVE people and will go far out of my way to avoid offending anyone. Sometimes that in itself offends people."* ~Rachel

## Self-Conscious

I am an extremely self-conscious person.

It's not that I care all too much what others think of me. As I get older, I put less and less stock in the judgments of others. But that does not stop me from being self-conscious in everyday conversation.

When I am interacting with someone, I am hyper aware of each little movement that I make, every blemish on my face, every minute change in my mask. The reason for this is my tuned in focus to the feelings of others.

People react to a million different things each day, usually within a blip of a moment. Many of these things are hardly consciously recognizable or memorable to the individual themselves, but in the moment, I feel each of those minute responses. So when I smile, I feel the response immediately to that smile. When I use the wrong word, I feel the brief confusion. When I scratch my nose, I feel the momentary disgust. I feel each tiny little nuance of the other person's reactions.

Allow me to put it into a non-empathic perspective: Let's say you are having a conversation with someone, and that person verbally, immediately and bluntly picks apart each thing that you do. They call you out on improper word use. They tell you anything you do that makes them uncomfortable, angry, happy, excited. They critique any piece of your physical appearance they may notice. They tell you *everything* they are thinking about you, truthfully and unabashedly.

I would imagine that less than two minutes into interacting with that person you would become quite self-conscious. And every conversation with them after that, you would worry about anything you said or did.

That is how it is for an INFJ in each conversation. But we can't read minds, we can only feel feelings. So when someone reacts instinctually to something, no matter how irrational or unjustified it may be, and even if that feeling is just in an instant and fades from their conscious and subconscious immediately, I still noticed it and I still wonder about it.

This has some upsides. It turns INFJs into chameleons because it makes it easy for us to fit in with any type. We can cater to those around us in tone, actions and words, without them even noticing our fabrications. If we say the wrong thing or offend someone, we know in a moment and can quickly recover the situation. On the more negative side, it is also what makes us so great at manipulating others.

It's certainly exhausting and frustrating. I long to be one of those people who can cast aside the thoughts of others and just be 100% themselves in every situation. It seems peaceful, easy and freeing. But try as I might, practice as I may, I can never quite get there. No matter how my confidence builds, I cannot escape the screaming feelings of the everyday reactions of others. Just another day in the life of an INFJ.

## Words from Other Rare Minds

*"It feels like you see life through a magnifying glass and feel everything so raw and amplified and everyone else lives with a buffer to their feelings. Being an INFJ for me is like living with raw nerves." ~Anonymous*

*"Naked, exposed and scrutinized. And an internal storm of emotions that is hard to grasp."* ~N.

# Jealousy

I am an extremely jealous person. If I see anyone who is better than me at anything in any way, my jealous side shines strong.

I hold myself accountable for my jealousy in that I never tear others down or get angry with them for their success. It is easy for me to feel their pride and joy when they succeed so I do feel proud of them and for them. I like to help others become better in every way that I can, so tearing them down would go against all for which I stand.

That being said, I still feel my own jealousy. This jealousy stems more from my failures than their successes. Because of my constant desire to be perfect, when I see someone who is better at something than I am, it is like a mirror back to me showing me that I am not yet perfect and still obviously have room for improvement.

I welcome this jealousy. It is the fuel that helps me constantly improve.

If I see someone who is in great physical shape compared to myself, it motivates me to eat right and exercise. If I see a successful blog or an accomplished writer, it helps me focus harder on my writing and do anything I can to improve it. As a mother, I like to read about and surround myself with wonderful parents so I can learn from them to be the best mother I can be.

It is also for this reason that I strongly dislike when people use social forums to complain, admit their shortfalls, or look for comrades in failure. These people seem to be seeking emotional comfort in areas that they are not succeeding rather than looking at the truth of their failures and trying to improve themselves. I much prefer to hear of the successes and proud stories of others.

Many people look at jealousy as a bad trait. I disagree. I think jealousy itself is a wonderful gift of humankind that can help us to be better in all that we do. If, however, we lose personal accountability, then jealousy is warped into negative feelings that harm those around us.

I know, as always, I am rare but I do love my jealousy. I love my accountability. I love that I am always trying to improve.

## Words from Other Rare Minds

*"In the Jungian world, envy (which has a lot of semantic overlap with jealousy) is a diagnostic marker for the 'bright shadow.' Most of us are familiar with the psychological term 'shadow side' as referring to negative aspects of ourselves that we are not conscious of or have repressed. The 'bright shadow' refers to the positive version: when we're envious of someone, a Jungian would say that it's because we carry the unexpressed potential in ourselves for some version of the quality we envy." ~Barbara*

# Accountability

I think a lot about accountability. I hold myself accountable for quite a bit...almost everything, really. Even things that are probably not my fault cause me great guilt and self-reflection. If something goes wrong, if someone is unhappy or if I have personally failed, I spend a great deal of time wondering how I could have done better, how I can improve myself and how I can fix the situation in the future.

Without personal accountability we cannot grow nor can we ever improve ourselves.

I find that this trait is lacking in most people which saddens and frustrates me. So often people fail and manage to turn it away from themselves by blaming or belittling others.

There are tons of websites out there devoted to sharing your personal failures in order to make others feel better. How awful is that? How does that help us grow? Instead, I believe it gives us an "out." A way to accept our imperfections guilt-free. How then do we grow? How do we improve? How do we prevent failure in the future?

Many times I feel that my accomplishments have been belittled in order to make someone else avoid personal accountability. I am a very honest person. What you see is always me.

For example, I am a writer. I write about areas in which I am successful (though I can always still improve). I have had cases when someone reads my writing, feels inferior or poorly about themselves and then turns to calling me a liar. They say that I must be purposely hiding my faults, staging my life and forging a persona that does not truly exist. They belittle my accomplishments and make me seem worse in order to avoid looking at the true reason of my success (hard work and dedication) and why they failed. I have dealt with these situations through all areas of my life.

No, I am not saying I am perfect. There have been many cases when I read another's writing and feel inferior. I mope for a moment about why I cannot be as successful or great as them. But I look at *why* I am not as successful as them. I figure out what I can do to get to their level, and perhaps become better. I recognize that they are, in fact, better than me in that area and that I need to better myself. I never insult them, belittle them or bring them down. They have done nothing wrong. The fault is with me and my emotions. I use my envy to improve, not to destroy myself or those around me.

We all have areas in which we succeed and fail. It is just life. It is what makes us become better people. But if we take those failures and accept them…or worse, glorify them…then we will only suffer personally.

Discussing your faults is acceptable and human. Not coming up with a solution or method of improvement will lead to your own further suffering and failure. Tearing down others to make yourself feel better is juvenile and will lead to your downfall.

As INFJs, we feel we must always improve. We hold ourselves accountable in order to become better. We lift up others to lift up ourselves. We do not hide from our faults, but rather we face them head on.

Accountability makes me incredibly proud to be an INFJ. This quality alone makes the rest of the burdens we bear seem worth it, for I know, in the end, I will triumph and I will help others triumph as well.

# Section Two

# The Struggles

# Fight

I find I fight with my thoughts daily.

My mind is such a jumbled place, filled with many thoughts, emotions, memories, ponderings and more. These thoughts are not always pleasant as the world around me is filled with so much negativity. When I hear an unpleasant story or feel one's unhappy emotions, they stick with me for a long time, even if I try to shut them out.

For that reason, I often have to fight to keep negative thoughts from entering my mind. By thoughts, I mean recalling horrible stories and emotions and keeping my incredibly vivid imagination at bay.

When I see a news story about a missing persons case, my mind runs wild in many directions of what may have happened to that person. I often fear my intuition is accurate. I worry that I can conjure up so many awful scenarios. I dread that the thought of each scenario I create will stay with me for some time.

Even though these scenarios are fabricated within my own mind, the emotions that come with them are real. For example, if I am told someone lost a kitten, I conjure up a television-like image in my mind of that pet being hit by a vehicle. Along with that thought, I feel the emotions of the cat (fear, pain, dread, confusion) as well as the emotions of the person who ran over the cat and those of the owner when they discover the body. While none of what I am thinking may have actually happened, I still have to grieve through it and fight with the emotions of it, all of which will stay with me for years to come.

Some people like to tell stories of negative things in the world, sugar-coating portions or leaving them out entirely. But by hearing the bare bones of a story, my mind runs wild and the damage is done. I now have to live with those thoughts and emotions for a long time (possibly forever), never diminishing or fading. They constantly enter my mind fresh, often uncontrollably, and I have to fight the thoughts to the back burner of my brain.

I am an overall happy person but I struggle daily with negativity and pain. Each day I must take on with a guarded mind and closed emotions. Sometimes I can handle it strong and brave, while other times I wish I could crumble under the weight of the emotional pain.

My mind is very active and exhausting. I actually have moments of great pride when I recognize how strong I must be to handle all which dwells within me.

## Words from Other Rare Minds

*"My imagination is way too good and my mind is way too stubborn to just be able to turn it off. I have to feel my way through its entirety before I'm able to find my center again, and that's not always an overnight process."* ~M.

# Roller Coaster

Every second of every day I exist on a roller coaster. My emotions are never consistent for any period of time…and by period of time, I mean my emotions fluctuate from "so happy I want to burst" to "longing to retreat into a cave of despair and cry uncontrollably" within a matter of minutes.

My mind is always so full of emotions because I can hold onto anything that I have ever felt forever, and that includes the emotions of others. When I hold onto those emotions, they are as fresh as the moment they occurred. Every emotion is so vivid in my mind that I constantly overflow with Niagara-like waterfalls of joy, contentment, rage, fear, depression and every combination thereof.

The perfectionism that I so strongly feel the need to achieve only makes it worse. I want to be the best out there. I want to be the wife every man dreams of, the housewife every woman longs to be, the parent that is asked to write books about child-rearing, and the person that everyone wants to lay friendship claim to. When I see anyone better at anything, I crumble. Needless to say, this happens frequently.

I can lock myself in my house and dwell on all the positive things in my existence and bring myself higher emotionally than anyone I know. I can overflow with joy about the numerous things in my life that I know I am good at. I can enter the world with a self-esteem level beyond your comprehension. Then, in a moment, I'm nothing. The world hits me and I realize my imperfections. I realize someone doesn't like my writing. I realize someone thinks my child is rude. I realize someone doesn't like *me*.

My emotions exhaust me every day and yet I never let it show. I never let people see the pain, but I want them to see the joy. This makes me come across very fake, which is another thing that may make someone not like me, furthering my realization that I am imperfect and have a long way to go before I ever reach my goals.

I may be in daily pain…but I am also in daily joy.

I may be imperfect…but I know I am enough.

I may be cursed with a constant emotional roller coaster…but I know that I am gifted because I am an INFJ.

# Anxiety

While I am not sure if anxiety is common for all INFJs, I know it plays a very prominent role in my life *because* I am an INFJ.

I go through periods in my life where I worry to the point of shutting down and sometimes leading to depression if I do not catch it soon enough. I tend to be a very self-aware person, though I can easily hide from myself by becoming enveloped in the emotions of others. That is when my anxiety is more likely to morph into depression.

I have General Anxiety Disorder (GAD) which is the most common type of anxiety experienced by millions of people daily. While anxiety and depression are daily struggles for me, I am successful in managing myself and overcoming both struggles as they begin to overtake me.

My reason for suffering from GAD is my constant desire to achieve perfection in my life. I am always worried that I am failing and it is difficult to talk myself out of my negative thoughts. Often times, I need the input of an outside source (usually my husband) to help me see logically. As a "Feeling" personality, logic can usually escape me.

My anxiety worsens when there is something in my life in which I feel it particularly important to succeed. My typical areas of anxiety are mothering, marriage and my writing. You will notice that each one of these things requires me to meet the expectations of others. Since I am not yet perfect in any category, I feel I fail their expectations, turn to worrying excessively, and eventually am overcome with constant anxiety.

To combat this I focus on natural methods like diet changes, exercise, faith, and natural supplements. This is a strong battle for me but I take heart in knowing I *will* win it because I *have* to be successful in my life. Knowing that GAD is an obstacle makes me very determined to win against it.

My desire to always be better may cause my anxiety and depression, but it is also a blessing that helps me overcome it daily. Yet another noticeable oxymoron of an INFJ's existence.

# Manipulation

While many aspects of the INFJ personality type tend to shed a consistently good and selfless light, there is one not-so-good area that we, whether or not we are aware of it, are masters of: Manipulation.

Because of our unique ability to read other people, even people we know nothing about, INFJs know just what to say or do to make people give us exactly what we want. We can read their body language, emotions and words much deeper than other personality types which allows us to know what we need to do to manipulate each individual.

When I was a child, I would often manipulate my parents into doing what I wanted or giving me what I wanted. I did not realize at the time exactly what I was doing, but when it was over I would always feel a slight pang of guilt. Now that I am grown, have studied psychology and sociology and have learned about myself and my personality, I realize exactly what I was doing and am completely aware of it when I do it today.

The kicker is that manipulating someone else is the only negative thing we can do to those around us that does not hurt ourselves. When we manipulate someone, that person is left giving us what we wanted without any remorse and negative emotions towards us because we have tricked them into thinking it is the right thing. Because of that, we do not feel any negativity from them, but only their positive emotions.

The only thing that prevents me from manipulating people is my awareness of what I am doing and the knowledge that it is wrong and immoral. If you have an INFJ with very little established morality, they may not feel the guilt of manipulating others which is when this power could really hurt those around them.

The art of manipulation is a very slippery slope for INFJs. The key to keeping it in check is to constantly be aware of ourselves in every conversation. Because it is a technique that comes effortlessly to us, we must use caution and not slip into the dishonest method of using our unique abilities to get what we want.

To those who are not INFJs but who do know someone who is, I can almost guarantee you that they have manipulated you in some way, shape or form. Sometimes we just do it because we do not catch ourselves in time. You will probably never realize you have been manipulated by an INFJ because, I hate to admit it, we *are* that good.

# Protection

There are many different kinds of introverts out there and they are all introverts for their own reasons.

My husband is an ISTJ. He is an introvert mostly because he just doesn't care. He never feels he needs to explain or prove himself. He never has a desire to tell people about what is in his mind. When asked a direct personal question, he will never lie, but he will not offer much information. He is an introvert and he is completely content with that.

I, as an INFJ, fall on the opposite side of the introvert spectrum. I am not content with being an introvert. When asked a direct personal question, I will often give too much information. I have a constant longing for people to know everything about me, from my favorite color to how my mind works. By the way, my favorite color is red.

Then why am I an introvert? Protection.

After a lifetime of putting pieces of myself out there only to be misunderstood, judged, mocked and humiliated, I learned that my unique mind needs to be protected. Others often fail to understand me, so it is easier on myself to just close the door to my brain. Yet, I still long to have deep and meaningful relationships with everyone I encounter, so I truly wish I could open up to everyone around me.

My husband is an honest person who just has no interest in telling you about his mind. He often times doesn't even think about it or realize it. INFJs, however, are secretive. We are selective in what we will share. We are completely aware of what we withhold from others.

I am a very different personality to everyone I meet. It is not that I am being maliciously two-faced or deceitful, but rather I offer information about myself based on what the person can handle. It protects my mind. If I share the wrong information, I feel how it makes them uncomfortable, anxious, confused or angry. It is better for both of us if I just withhold certain information about myself.

There is a lot inside the mind of an INFJ. We are never at peace in our brains. We are always thinking.

Our minds are constantly active. We intuitively know things that we cannot explain. We work through every human encounter with a fine-toothed comb. Trust me. It is just easier for us to keep most of that to ourselves.

## Words from Other Rare Minds

*"We have such an inner NEED to be known and accepted...so we ration it out in small amounts to people, intuitively waiting to see if they can handle a bit more...or not. Isn't it really our deepest desire to open the floodgates and in that most vulnerable moment to be completely known, understood, loved, and valued? That is my dream...to just be able to be completely myself and feel safe." ~Anonymous*

*"I will tell my whole life story to anyone who wants to hear it. A complete stranger even. They may end up knowing more about me than a close friend or family member. It all depends on if they 'get it' and if they can handle it. INFJ emotions can be a bit intense and other personalities think we are being dramatic or they are*

*freaked out by it. Better off keeping it all to myself and avoid the negative reactions."* ~I.

# Shut Down

Despite my ability to constantly feel on a level much deeper than any other personality type, I also have an interesting ability to shut down emotionally. This shut down is usually very brief but, I believe, very necessary.

INFJs feel *a lot*. I cannot stress enough how much we feel. Sometimes it blows my mind to realize how much feeling capacity I actually have. I feel my own emotions. I feel the emotions of everyone around me. I feel emotions of people I have heard about. I feel the emotions of people driving by me on the interstate. I feel emotions from my past, as well as the pasts of others, as vividly as though they were happening right now. I feel *everything*.

Because of this, I can get overwhelmed both mentally and physically and I need a break to protect my mind. This is when I shut down. I temporarily block out all emotions around me and I suppress my own emotions.

Sometimes I can choose to shut down and other times it happens involuntarily. Choosing to shut down is difficult because it first comes with guilt. I always feel guilty ignoring the emotions around me. I feel like I have turned off my most important purpose, particularly because it usually happens when I am probably most needed (for example, when a loved one is deeply hurting and needs my support). It is like a surgeon walking out in mid-surgery or a therapist turning their back on a suicidal patient. So to choose to shut down is very difficult for me. It is one of the very few selfish things of which I am capable, but I still must deal with the painful emotions it causes me, both before and after the shut down.

The involuntary moments are more common, especially when life gets hard. I can emotionally shut down and not even realize it. I walk through life in a numbed state, performing the appropriate tasks while wearing a mask.

Usually the emotional shut downs last only moments, just long enough for my mind to reset and to help me cope with the situation. But sometimes those moments turn into days, then months, then years. This is when I fall into depression.

Depression for me, as well as many other INFJs, is numbness. It is when I no longer care to feel for those around me nor for myself. It is nothing more than a long term shut down.

Overall, I feel these shut downs are a blessing to an INFJ. We need a break from all that we bear. Even those shut downs that come at incredibly inopportune times come about for a reason. The short breaks are what help us get through life. It only becomes a curse when it turns into a long term shut down.

Yet another aspect of us that shows its face as a blessing as well as a curse.

Section Three

# Everyday Living

# Physical World

Sometimes I forget I have a body.

My physical being is frequently pushed to the back burner. I live inside my mind, focusing only on feelings, ideas and fantasies. I see others and am aware of their feelings, intentions and purpose. The physical realm seems pointless to me, like something that exists as an obstacle or inconvenience to the greater picture of what really matters.

This is usually why I have to work so hard at my mask. It acts as a superficial requirement of others in order to get to the next layer, the spiritual layer within which I truly exist.

Sometimes I reach the point of exhaustion with physically being. The actions of movement and gestures wear me down. It is not a matter of laziness. I am actually a very physically fit person. Rather, it is a matter of priority. Going out for coffee, heading to a doctor's appointment, nodding to passers-by, or making dinner are all far lower on my priority list than pondering, dreaming, fantasizing, learning, feeling and inquiring.

Of course, that is not to say I completely dislike physical activity. I actually enjoy it to some extent. I love to hug my children, kiss my husband, exercise regularly and type away at a keyboard, but they are all means to a spiritual end. Physical necessities that biologically release endorphins, oxytocin and other hormones to improve my spiritual and emotional needs. I am not averse to or ignorant of the benefits of the physical world, it is just such a low priority to me that I can actually forget about it.

For example, I can pick up a good book and sit for hours, forgetting to eat, drink, use the bathroom or even readjust my body to alleviate soreness and achieve greater physical comfort because the book sends me so deep into my mind that my physical sense no longer matters.

This baffles my introverted sensing (Si) husband (ISTJ). It can lead me to neglect my health until it is too late, just because I do not realize something is wrong. After much self-reflection, it can even cause me to question my own sanity. I can become so far removed from the physical world that I actually wonder whether or not I am even a part of it.

In fact, the Si function is considered the eighth cognitive function of an INFJ, making it the last priority even in the technical sense. Some speculate that the INFJ is the only personality type to actually only have seven functions because we tend to lack any negative or positive attributes of introverted sensing (Si), leading some to believe that we do not have the capacity for that function. Fascinating to ponder, though not really my area of expertise.

But if you are an INFJ who has ever felt "other-worldly," wondered the purpose to your physical sense or just plain become frustrated with having to attend to physical human needs, recognize that you are not alone. We are not insane. As always, we are just extremely different from most of this world...this very physical world.

# Words

My words are my soul.

Whether I am writing or speaking, my words are always the most accurate window into what I really think, feel and believe. I have never understood lies, games, rumors or gossip. Words, in my world, are always pure.

It frustrates me immensely when people do not believe my words and frustrates me even more when they misinterpret them. Often times people will think I mean something completely off base because my mask fails me. Perhaps my tone of voice was off or my facial expression seemed forced. Maybe my words could be taken in many ways and the listener chose not to give me the benefit of the doubt.

Whatever the situation, it shakes me to the core when I am misunderstood or misinterpreted. My soul feels wounded and offended when someone questions my words, words which seemed so pure to me.

It is rare in writing that my words are taken the wrong way. It usually only happens when I write quickly and do not proofread. But in person or over the phone, my words are, more often than not, misinterpreted. I struggle with speaking on the fly. I tend to panic when a response is desired immediately (as is the case in most conversation).

When I feel forced to speak without proper reflection, I can get frustrated, and sometimes angry. I feel as though I am being robbed of the opportunity to share the complete truths that I feel. I often want to explain myself further but rarely does the listener have the patience except for those closest to me.

In their defense, I want to speak at great length even about the tiniest things. When asked if I enjoyed the meatloaf, I want to be sure my answer is as thorough and honest as possible, when most people only desire and have the patience for a simple yes or no.

To me, words serve a great purpose and should never be spoken just to fill silence. Words are gold and have immense power. My words define me through and through.

My words are my soul.

# Simple

I crave simplicity.

I work very hard to keep things in my world very simple. Other than writing, I am unemployed. I make my food from scratch. My home is scarcely (though I believe beautifully) decorated. My days are void of strict schedules or appointments. I limit my time online, avoid the phone unless necessary and never watch the news.

Though people may judge this choice of lifestyle, it is what brings me inner joy and peace. I am able to meditate on my faith often and refocus myself from all negative thoughts (though they still enter my mind).

The world is active and high-paced. As a Highly Sensitive Person (HSP), I can become easily overwhelmed and emotionally exhausted by trying to live the life of the extroverted society in which I live.

It took me quite a long time to realize this. I used to try to keep up with all those who called me weird or reclusive, but I now recognize that my simple lifestyle is where my joy resides. As an INFJ and HSP, I believe it is impossible to reach my full potential in a hectic life. I need peace, calm and tranquility to handle all the activity that goes on within my mind.

If you are an INFJ, I strongly recommend that you simplify. Forget what society tells you. Ignore the judgments of your reclusive nature (though difficult, it grows easier to not care what those around you think). Rearrange your life to find peace and joy. Meditate and ensure quiet and alone time. We all need breaks and we need periods of voluntary emotional shut down.

Most importantly, recognize that peace is possible despite being an INFJ. Not only is it possible, but I believe we are able to achieve a level of peace unknown to so many around us.

Though it took me many years to become confident about myself, I love being an introvert. I love my reclusive style. I love my simple life.

# Change

I love change…

…when it is well thought out, gradual, planned, justified and, most importantly, on my terms.

Any change that is hasty, pointless and out of my control can send me into overly-emotional bouts of anxiety that make me wish I could shut down and lock myself in a dark, non-stimulating room until I am able to regain control of my world.

As an INFJ, I often feel that my intuition leads me to always know what is best for those around me. Because of this, I tend to be a control freak. I am adamant about change for the purpose of improvement and progress towards perfection. But any change I encourage has been bouncing around my mind for some time while I ponder every aspect and purpose. I never make hasty decisions and I certainly do not jump in headfirst and without deep contemplation and planning. Only when I am certain the change is for the better do I follow through with it.

When change happens that is outside of my control, my mind still needs to complete the mulling process. I need to absorb the change, dwell on every aspect of it and decide whether or not it is for the best. If I conclude that the change is good, I accept it and happily move on. If it is not good, I work on ways to fix it that are within my control. However, until I have had an appropriate amount of time to go through this process, I will panic. I will feel overstimulated, overwhelmed and anxious, especially if the change requires any action on my part.

I have read many articles on how to accept change, how to deal with unexpected situations and how to release control, but with each article, I come to the same conclusion: this is who I am and it is not changeable.

I kept trying to figure out how to change my need for control but it was only when I embraced it as an ingrained part of who I am that I could accept it, deal with it and live with it.

When change outside of my control occurs, I allow myself to emotionally freak out. I allow myself that moment of anger, fear and anxiety. To rob myself of it only makes me worse. Everyone has coping processes, and this is mine. As long as the emotions do not take over my life completely, there is no harm in allowing myself to feel them in the moment.

    I love change. I feel I know best. I am an emotional person. I am okay with, and am proud of, every part of that.

## Words from Other Rare Minds

*"I adjust to change...but it's gradual. Like many introverts, I need to walk away, think it through alone and implement." ~Stephen*

*"I tend to like certain types of change - when I've mulled it over in my head and decided that change was necessary for my growth. But if change is thrust upon me without giving me time to process it - and most especially when it requires immediate action on my part - I freak out and panic very easily." ~L.*

# Procrastination

Despite the fact that I am "Judicial," I can be considered lazy. I know this flaw is in me. I hate it. But I also understand why it is there.

As an INFJ, I am an extreme perfectionist. I believe that perfection is something that we should always strive for and I spend every second of the day trying to achieve that goal. Needless to say, that is a pretty large goal that can wear me out in an instant. Thus, I procrastinate.

I will look at a project that needs to be done, realize how much work it will take to do it perfectly and wind up exhausting myself before I have even begun. It does not matter how large or how small the project is. I feel I must be perfect in everything.

For example, I always procrastinate when it comes to vacuuming my house. The perfectionist in me thinks that every time I vacuum, I should get every square inch of the floors, including crevices and under furniture. Because that would take quite a bit of time and energy, I just do not vacuum at all. I would rather not do anything than do something half-heartedly.

This serves to be a double-edged sword since, by procrastinating, I know that I am not reaching perfection in myself. I then feel I must tackle everything right away, realize how much energy that will sap from me since being perfect at everything is really hard work, and thus, I am back to doing nothing which means I am back to being imperfect.

This is yet another daily exhausting character trait that causes the mind of an INFJ to never be at peace.

## Words from Other Rare Minds

*"Whenever assigned to do some kind of activity, I either leave it completely untouched or completely finished."*
~Cilla

# Shopping

I love shopping...for about fifteen minutes.

I get very excited about going on a shopping trip. The idea of browsing the aisles, window shopping and people-watching all make me look forward to an afternoon out. It always starts out well and I feel the thrill I am sure many Sensors feel on a shopping trip.

But it does not take long for me to get worn out. The over-abundance of people, especially if they are rude or angry. All the lights, music and sounds. The overwhelming visual stimulations of brightly colored displays covered in signs of varying labels for prices, sales and clearances. The zig-zagging aisles, center displays, dangling signs, confusing layouts. Nothing consistent from department to department or store to store. Intercom announcements, squeaky cart wheels, dinging registers, crying babies.

All these external stimulations while trying to focus on the task at hand: purchasing an item. Price comparing, number crunching, tag reading, percentage calculating and quick decisions based on personal budgeting. Add in other possible factors like time constraints, conversations with a shopping companion or extroverted passer-by, bad weather dampening your clothes or chilling your bones, hunger from an approaching meal.

Throw it all together and what seems like a leisurely outing of which most people seek for pleasure becomes an overstimulation nightmare that can leave me mentally incapacitated for days.

Explaining this to the average person leaves them questioning my sanity and throwing out terms like "agoraphobia" and "social anxiety." This, however, is not the case. I have no fears or anxieties about shopping. I just become so overstimulated and overwhelmed by a world designed for those who enjoy their senses being constantly aroused that I become as exhausted as the average introvert would from a six hour one-on-one conversation with Tony Robbins.

Yes, I can handle it. I shop regularly when I need to, some trips going better than others, but each time I will require some time to emotionally shut down. I may even end the trip hovering my ESTP shadow.

And after a few days I will psych myself up again about all the exciting prospects of a shopping trip and may even start to once again believe that I love shopping.

# Telephone Aversion

My family loves to talk. They call me often (sometimes daily) just to talk about random happenings during their day.

I rarely call them. I call them when I have something important to say. If I have nothing to say, I feel no reason to call.

As an introvert, I hate talking on the phone. As an INFJ, it is my least effective form of communicating. Verbal words are not my strong suit. Writing comes easily to me and I can make sure I am conveying the correct meaning prior to hitting "publish." Speaking one-on-one in person is also not necessarily challenging to me because I can gauge the feelings of others, read facial expressions, observe body language, and note any small physical responses to my words.

Over the phone, I just have a voice. A lot can be concealed, so I have a hard time figuring out how the person on the other end is responding to my words.

Because of this, talking on the phone, even about petty topics, can quickly exhaust me emotionally.

Yet, I find when I express this to those who call me often, they take it personally and become offended. I by no means wish to offend, so I promptly retract my words and continue to suffer in silence from daily phone calls, hoping to have a good enough excuse to avoid them more often than not.

I would venture to say most introverts dislike talking on the phone. We tend to spend time in our own heads, thinking over what has been said to us, mulling around what has happened throughout our day, then speaking when necessary. When someone calls frequently, we are robbed of the time to be inside our minds to appropriately account for our day. Cell phones make this even more of a problem because of the constant connection to anyone with our phone number.

If you are an extrovert, or if you are an introvert who happens to enjoy talking on the phone, please respect those who need some time alone. Don't take it personally. That person does still care for you deeply, we just do not have much too say.

## Words from Other Rare Minds

*"My cell phone is perpetually on silent mode because I just can't stomach the thought of dealing with incoming phone calls. Calling out is even worse - I avoid that like the plague. I would much rather write/email someone than call them."* ~L.

*"I keep my phone on silent most of the time because hearing it ring gives me a mini panic attack. I like to rehearse what I'm going to say in my head before I make a call...I am horrible at verbally expressing myself and if I don't have something rehearsed, I will sound like a blubbering idiot."* ~I.

# Social Media

Social media is like my daily answered prayer meets my daily hell.

I often hear that INFJs are walking oxymorons in that most of us crave, rather *need*, frequent human interaction and yet we also need time to ourselves. To an INFJ, solitary confinement would be the worst form of torture. We live for people. We live for everyone around us.

That being said, people affect us very deeply in that we feel everything they feel, live everything they live, and struggle through everything they struggle through. Being near people robs us of being ourselves because we wind up very focused on being them, fixing them and pleasing them.

Finding a balance between our needed socialization and our needed seclusion is a daily struggle for many.

Social media offers us the perfect platform to reach so many people and have human interaction at our fingertips whenever we crave it. Yet, it also thrusts us into a 24/7 life of dealing with people.

For me, this turns into a blessing and a curse (as much of my life could be described). While I want to "friend" everyone I have ever met and learn as much as I can about them, with that comes the obligation to do as much as I can for everyone I find on social media at every moment. Someone is always suffering. That is the existence of humankind. Social media just causes me to be aware of that daily and makes me feel obligated to fix it.

I have realized that I cannot help everyone and by attempting to do so, it distracts me from helping those that I can. Because of this, I frequently go through my social media profiles and remove people from my lists. This helps me remove those of whom I was really not interacting with anyways. All their presence did was cause me daily anxiety in that I could not help them but I longed to.

My connections are kept at a manageable amount which, while not completely releasing me from my anxiety, makes me a more productive member of the social media community. I can see more status updates of those on my list. I can become more familiar with their lives, including every up and down of their posted day. I can reach out and help those in need and have actually sent personal messages to those who need more personal attention.

I still feel like I am constantly submerged in the 24/7 socialization of today's society which can exhaust me, but at least I am now seeing a benefit from my exhaustion. At least I am now focusing on personal relationships rather than trying to save the world.

I believe that INFJs are special. We are here for a bigger purpose and many of us are constantly trying to find perfection to reach that purpose. But even Jesus Himself did not reach the entire world immediately. Even He worked one person at a time.

## Words from Other Rare Minds

*"We can't help everyone, and if we try no one really gets what they should have. We spread ourselves too thin and lose sight of the things that are truly important to us, like*

*being us and trying to understand our own thoughts instead of spending that time understanding others."*
~Wendy

*"I have a love-hate relationship with Facebook. I have de-friended and re-friended an embarrassing number of times. I am torn between the desire to help and the intuition to protect (i.e. my family, my privacy, authenticity of relationships)."* ~L. M.

# Helping

It was a regular shopping trip, just picking up a few family necessities. I stood before the wall of produce, comparing prices and finally deciding on cucumbers (a steal for the week) when I saw the old man beside me gently placing the wrapped lettuce back on its stack. He hunched slightly over the cart which temporarily housed his cane. I could easily see the large boot on his foot that caused his clearly painful stature adding misery to an already deteriorating body.

"Ma'am?" He stood about a foot shorter than me as he gazed up like a lost child. "Do you know what cabbage looks like? My wife sent me shopping and I never do it."

I smiled and walked him over to the cabbage. With a "you're welcome" and a polite nod, I mosied back to my cart. The completion of a simple good deed that would leave most satisfied to aid an elder, and yet my heart ached.

I could see so much more behind his words. I sensed a gentle lie covering a truth he was too scared to say aloud. Perhaps his wife was hospitalized and nearing the end. Or maybe he had already lost her. I am not sure of his full story, but I know his words were masking a complete truth.

I moved along to the next aisle, more focused on my thoughts than the shelves before me. I wished I had done more for him. Showing him the cabbage seemed not enough. I longed to ask if he needed more help. To finish his shopping for him, purchase his goods and drive him home. Perhaps schedule a weekly shopping assistance. I ached to clean his house, iron his shorts, make his breakfast the way he likes it. To fill the role of the wife for whom he was so clearly aching. The woman upon which he survived. The woman who could no longer fill the role he fell in love with and longed to have again.

With each item I removed from the shelf, my heart grew heavier. I yearned to search the store for him. To hold him while he cried. To be a safe place for his manly pride to shatter.

But as I completed my purchase, I knew I would never see him again. I knew it was not my place to pick up the pieces and help him move forward. I knew it was a burden my heart would now carry forever.

But I took a small amount of comfort in knowing I was there to help him find the cabbage. And while *I* wanted to help him so much more, maybe, just maybe, that is where *he* needed to start.

## Words from Other Rare Minds

*"I was in Wal-Mart a couple of months ago, shopping for some groceries, and the store was packed. An older man walked up to me (lots of people he could have asked but he gravitated towards me) and asked me how to make a pack of instant fettuccini noodles. I told him to boil water and add a little butter. He thanked me and quickly walked off. I knew right then that he could not read. I just stood there, crying. I wanted to help him read. I wanted to go over to his house every afternoon and teach him how. I wanted to help him so much. I made it to the next aisle, trying my best to shove that*

*sadness down. I hate that. I'm so tired. I'm so tired of feeling and knowing. I'm so tired of being sad."*
*~Belinda*

# Passions

My passions drive me...

...but they also break me.

I spend my time in two alternating mental states: under-stimulated and overwhelmed. When I am under-stimulated, I am ready to take on the world. All of my passions suddenly seem conquerable all at the same time. I am ready to write novels, commit to hours of community service, lead committees and make way too many promises.

Then I become overwhelmed. The many commitments destroy my alone time, drain me mentally and can sometimes trigger my anxieties. All of this puts me in a negative and hopeless state that has me feeling discouraged and like I will never be able to do everything I was meant to for this world.

The simple solution seems to be finding a happy balance: finally landing in that perfect middle ground that allows me to happily and productively make a difference, one priority at a time. It sounds so possible, so rational, as I write it.

And yet, I do not. I hesitate to say that I *cannot*. Perhaps with more years, wisdom and experience I will be able to master this seemingly insurmountable task of achieving contented balance while still fulfilling my greater purpose. But for now, I continue to overwhelm myself. I continue to let my overly optimistic, energetic and extroverted alter-ego trump my thoughtful, low-key, introverted persona each time it decides to show its charming face.

But, as exhausted as it may make me at times and as often as I may regret some commitments, it usually does result in some positive progress, making even a tiny dent in my greater purpose.

My passions drive me and, despite their illogical and unrealistic methods, what better force to propel personal, and even global, progress?

# Restless

Some days my soul feels restless. My mind, my heart, my entire being just can't stop. Whether I am busy at daily life or sitting idle and alone in my pajamas, it hits me like a tidal wave, taking over every fiber of my essence.

Adding more to my life does not calm it. Projects, both productive and unproductive, feel pointless. Discussions and writings feel hollow. Change seems necessary yet I cannot figure out what to change. This restlessness represents a longing in my spirit. A void that cannot be filled in this world. A calling to something greater, bigger, unknown to my earthly person.

I want to travel, but nowhere seems worth traveling. I want to learn, but all attainable knowledge feels worthless. I want to be, to exist, on a plane deeper and more profound than ever before. My spirit screams louder with each minute as if a piece of myself that I have yet to discover is thrashing wildly, trying to break free of a trap only this world has set for it.

In one moment, everything my senses can process appears gray, empty and shallow and in another moment, each particle of existence, each shade of color, each subtle movement explodes around me screaming as loudly as my spirit.

This piece of me is always there. Most of the time I can tame it, reduce the feeling down to a quiet voice in the distance. But when it arises, when it screams, when it wants to be known, this restless piece of me is almost unbearable. Excitement, passion, curiosity, longing, thrill, overwhelming explosions of energy and emotions.

I don't understand this restlessness, but for now I embrace it and its power and trust that it will lead my spirit where it needs to go, not fighting it, but existing within it until restlessness becomes the rest I have never before known.

# Accomplishments

I have accomplishments. Sometimes they are great accomplishments in my life. Other times they are as small as finally succeeding in opening a jar of jelly without my husband present to assist. I recognize that I have accomplished many things in my life and met many of my own goals.

The problem?

I cannot relish in this fact.

Most of the people I know, when they accomplish a task, relish in their accomplishments for a period of time, usually acceptable for the size of the feat. They use it to fuel them. They use it to improve their self-esteem and self-worth. They are happy and proud of themselves. It is wonderful to "feel" their emotions.

I only know such emotions through other people. When I accomplish something, I cannot focus on how wonderful the accomplishment was or how proud of myself I should be. Rather, I dwell on the fact that I am still not perfect and I could do better.

Logically, I know I should be proud of myself. I know I should delight in my accomplishments and recognize that my talents are paying off. When I succeed, my heart skips a beat with joy the moment I recognize I have reached another plateau in my life, but that excitement wears off in a matter of minutes and I find myself thinking, *How can I be better? How can I hit that next plateau of success?*

I am always looking forward and trying to improve myself. Nothing short of perfection satisfies me. This increases my anxiety level because I always see how much more I need to do to be better.

It helps immensely when others tell me why I should be proud of myself. It is almost as though I need permission from those around me to enjoy my accomplishments. My husband constantly reminds me of why I should be proud of my accomplishments. His words allow me to relish for a few more moments, but then I shift quickly back into thinking about what I can do to be better.

Like most areas of an INFJ mind, this is a blessing and a curse. The curse is the constant anxiety and inability to feel pride and self-worth. But the blessing is that I am always working to improve myself. I love to improve myself. I love knowing that I am always doing my best to make myself better for those around me. I suppose you could say I relish in that daily. Perhaps that is the only accomplishment that matters to me.

I never settle. I always strive to be the best. It is a slow process, but I hold strong to the idea that I will one day reach my goal of perfection. If I lose that ultimate goal, then what is the point to ever trying to be better?

# Overthink

I overthink *everything*.

I agonize over every detail of my life. I wonder constantly what image I convey to those around me. I think, think and rethink about every sentence I write. I replay over and over every conversation I have had.

When I speak with someone, I absorb a lot of information. I take in noises, smells, words, hidden meanings, emotions, logic, and every other aspect of my environment. That is a lot to compute in the moment, so I will spend days, sometimes weeks, processing the information of that conversation.

I fret over things I have said and wonder how they were taken. I long to speak to that person again and smooth over any possible misunderstandings or call attention to things I may have missed the first time around.

Sometimes I can feel wonderful after meeting with someone but after a few days of overthinking the encounter, I feel like I was not my best. I fear the other person does not like me. I worry that I did not convey the appropriate image. I think that I was not open enough about myself or that I was too open.

When I write, I agonize over every word. I rethink every comma. I consider each possible way the reader will take my point. It takes me a short time to write a piece but days to agonize over it after it is published. When I go back and reread it a week or two later, I want to edit, edit and edit some more because it is far from perfection.

Though this thought process of overthinking things in my life is ingrained deep within me, I have come a long way in coping with it. I have learned not to let the anxiety affect me. I have taught myself to focus on the facts and not dwell in the possibilities. But above all else, I have gained a deeper confidence in myself that has allowed me to let go of the worry of how I portray myself.

An INFJ has an inner world that is far beyond the understanding of anyone around us. Our intuition and knowledge is something that is near impossible to convey to others. Once I learned to let go of all that I cannot control, my inner world became peaceful.

I still struggle with this peace. I still struggle with letting go. I still struggle with proving myself in the extroverted society in which I live.

But ultimately, I have come to allow myself to overthink in order to improve in the future while letting go of the past. I have learned to use my trait to reach my ultimate goal of perfection. I have turned what I once thought was a curse into a blessing.

I love that I overthink everything.

# Blessing

I have mentioned quite a lot that being an INFJ is a blessing and a curse.

It is exhausting, lonely and confusing. To those who still do not understand themselves, it can feel much more like a curse.

When I began writing this journal, I felt that my abilities to feel others and my incredible intuition were torturous. While I did know happiness, I was constantly exhausted and anxious. Living in an extroverted society, I always fought against my born intuition and tried to become something that I was not.

In the two years that I have spent writing this, so much has changed. My views on myself and others have been altered drastically through self-reflection and understanding.

*Being an INFJ is a blessing.*

Is it still exhausting? Yes. Do I often feel lonely? Definitely. Are there still moments of confusion? Occasionally.

But I have recognized that my gifts of deep thought, strong feelings, self-reflection and astounding intuition bring about incredible moments of joy and peace.

If you are an INFJ and are struggling with your internal world, know that it is possible to achieve contentment. Your life will always be difficult, but your rewards can be greater than any other personality type can imagine.

First step...learn and accept yourself.

For more about living as an INFJ, please visit:
http://jennifersoldner.com